The Taizé Experience

BROTHER ROGER

The Taizé Experience

PHOTOGRAPHS BY VLADIMIR SICHOV

GEOFFREY
CHAPMAN
MOWBRAY

Vladimir Sichov was born in the Soviet Union and has lived in Paris since 1980. He works for the SIPA-PRESS photographic agency. He has published several books of photos and his work has appeared in various leading magazines in Europe and the United States: *Paris-Match*, *Newsweek*, *Life*, *People*, *Stern*, *Bunte* and *Vogue*.

The photographs on pages 28, 30 and 76–77 are by Jacques Houzel, Hans Lachmann and R. Ramírez, respectively. Some pictures of journeys and visits outside Europe come from Taizé.

The texts accompanying the pictures are selected from various publications by Brother Roger.

Geoffrey Chapman Mowbray
A Cassell imprint
Artillery House, Artillery Row, London SW1P 1RT, England

Original edition published 1989 as *Erlebnis Taizé*, © Verlag Herder Freiburg im Breisgau 1989
Translation © Ateliers et Presses de Taizé 1990

English-language edition first published 1990

British Library Cataloguing in Publication Data
Roger. *of Taizé*
    The Taizé experience.
    1. France. Taizé. Men's religious communities; Communauté
de Taizé
    1. Title   II. Sichov, Vladimir, *1945–*   III. Erlebnis
Taizé. *English*
    267′.23′094443

ISBN 0-264-67179-1

Colour reproduction: H. u. H. Schaufler, Freiburg
Typeset by Chapterhouse, The Cloisters, Formby, L37 3PX
Printed and bound in Germany by Freiburger Graphische Betriebe

The Taizé Experience

The pages of this book take us on a kind of journey along a hillside in Burgundy, France. It was here that Brother Roger, the founder of Taizé, came to live half a century ago.

Here we discover the community that he brought into being, made up of brothers from several continents and various denominations. By their prayer, their work, and their hospitality, the brothers form a parable of communion amidst the divisions of the Church and of the human family.

Here, we encounter young people from every corner of the earth. They have been flocking to this tiny village in their tens of thousands over the last thirty years. They come as part of their search for trust and commitment in their lives. Three times each day, they join together with the brothers for prayer in the Church of Reconciliation. Every day, they take part in meetings that give them the opportunity to search for the well-springs of faith. Their few days here are spent in very simple living conditions, sharing their questions and experiences with young people from other backgrounds and horizons. Out of this experience of deepening the inner life comes an ardent desire to live in solidarity with the entire human family, especially in those places where it is wounded.

A visit to Taizé leads on to discovering the well-springs of the 'Pilgrimage of Trust on Earth' that the community has been animating in recent years. This is a worldwide pilgrimage, moving ever farther across the continents, which, like this book, remains open-ended.

A Pilgrimage of
Trust on Earth

If Christ were not risen, we would not be here, gathered together for intercontinental meetings. Risen from the dead, he communicates life to us.

We are passionately searching for Christ, who is present for every human being. In order to make the earth a place fit to live in, he offers us the possibility of going forward in a pilgrimage of trust across the earth.

When I chose the village of Taizé, I was alone. The silence of the deserts strengthens the encounter with God. Alone with ourselves, are we not more sensitive to a mysterious presence alive within us?

On 20 August 1940, when I arrived in this human wasteland, there was nothing to suggest these days when so many young people would come to Taizé. And there are all those far away as well, especially those young people very dear to us who are reduced to silence, imprisoned, suffering because of Christ and the Gospel.

With all of them, with people from every part of the world, we are being called to a life that exceeds all our hopes.

There is one question we are often asked: why do so many young people from every continent come to Taizé? My brothers and I sometimes say: we really don't know why; God will tell us on the day we meet him face to face in the life of eternity.

When, every evening throughout the year, winter and summer, a few of us remain in the church after the common prayer to listen to young people with something to confide, one of our main concerns is this: what lies beneath their hearts? What is tying them up in knots? And then something still more important: what are their particular gifts? How can they discover them?

We know that they have not come here as tourists. If so, they would have come to the wrong address. Most of them have come with one and the same question: how can I understand God? How can I know what God wants for me?

The tiny Burgundy village of Taizé was inhabited mainly by elderly people when Brother Roger arrived there at the beginning of the Second World War. The twelfth-century Romanesque church was unused at that time. While he was still alone, he was hiding political refugees, mainly Jews, who were fleeing the Nazis. Since the end of the 1950s, young and not-so-young people have been coming from all directions to Taizé for a week of prayer and reflection.

When they arrive, the young people receive a brief explanation about the week-long meetings.

Each day Brother Roger and other brothers listen to young people one at a time.

In coming to Taizé, you are being received by brothers bound for their whole lives by monastic commitments. You have come to join other young adults from every continent in their searching, to go together with them to the living springs of God through prayer and the silence of contemplation.

The meetings take place in a small area. Three times each day, the bells call everyone to the common prayer in the Church of Reconciliation, which often has to be extended by large tents

'You who are here, be reconciled and discover in the Gospel the spirit of the Beatitudes: joy, simplicity, mercy. If a trusting heart were at the beginning of everything . . . and each day were God's today.'

You have come to Taizé to discover a meaning for your life. One of Christ's secrets is that he loved you first. That is the meaning of your life: to be loved for ever, to be clothed in God's forgiveness and trust as in a garment. In this way you can take the risk of giving your life.

Morning, noon and evening, people queue
for their meals. It is an opportunity to
continue discussions.

14

Every time I go on the roads near Taizé, I see young people coming and going and I am surprised to hear myself say: what trusting faces! Trust placed in them is rarely disappointed. It urges us onward.

I trust the intuitions of the young people from so many different lands who gather here, return home, search, pray, come back again. Yes, I would go to the ends of the earth if necessary, to the farthest reaches of the globe, to speak over and over again of my confidence in the younger generations.

Each year, the intercontinental meetings bring together young adults from a hundred different nations. Eastern Europeans, in ever greater numbers, and Western Europeans meet with young people from the other side of the world. Young Europeans pay the travel costs of those from the Southern continents.

My whole life long, my desire has been never to condemn. The essential, in the presence of another person, has always been to try and understand rather than be understood. And to understand, faces count even more than words.

Every human being is unique. In every person it is possible to see Christ's own face. Nothing has more beauty, then, than a face that a whole life of combat and struggle has rendered transparent. There are only beautiful faces, be they sad or radiant. My life is discerning in others what ravages them, what delights them; it lies in sharing the suffering and the joy of others.

Easter Sunday morning. Young people exchange the Easter greeting with Brother Roger.

Receiving along with my brothers so many young people at Taizé means being above all listeners to them, never spiritual mentors.

Yes, refuse to monopolize anyone at all for yourself. The Virgin Mary shows us a gesture of offering: she did not keep her Son for herself, she offered him to the world.

Life in Taizé is simple but festive.

You need so little to live, so little to welcome others. When you welcome, hospitality can be hindered rather than helped by abundance. Around your table, a festive spirit will shine through in simplicity. A sense of sharing will lead you to make your home a place of peace and caring. Being poor in spirit according to the Gospel means imaginatively arranging all things in creation's simple beauty. It is incompatible with cold austerity.

Simplifying and sharing does not mean opting for austerity. Simplify in order to live intensely, in the present moment: you will discover the joy of beng alive, so closely linked to joy in the living God. Simplify and share as a way of identifying with Christ Jesus, born poor among the poor.

Do not worry if you have very little to share—such weak faith, so few belongings. In the sharing of that little, God fills you to overflowing, inexhaustibly.

Children: such a joy and such a mystery in our lives! Who can tell all that they communicate, through gifts unknown to them and already placed in them by the Holy Spirit? They help us to understand something of the living God by the trust they place in us, by a few words or a question they address to us, so unexpected that they awaken us to a life in God.

Let the simple of heart rejoice, happy are those who have the heart of a child! They have within them all the things of God.

The spirit of childhood means first and foremost simplicity. It is also wholehearted trust and wonder. Though childhood certainly has no monopoly on trust, it does contain a measure of innocence which, if wounded, marks us for life. Every experience leaves its mark as on a slab of soft wax. For God human beings are sacred, consecrated, by the wounded innocence of their childhood.

A childlike spirit is clear-eyed candour. Far from being simplistic, it is lucid as well. Different aspects of a situation, positive elements as well as negative ones, are not foreign to it. It has nothing childish about it. It is imbued with maturity. It presupposes boundless courage.

All the generations can take part in the intercontinental meetings. Many families spend a week in Taizé in the summer. Each day, during the common prayer, children come forward with candles in their hands to light the wicks of an oil lamp placed on a lampstand. While they are doing this, a chant is sung to celebrate the light of Christ. This symbol came from Asia.

Thinking about my imminent departure to go to spend time in a poor region of the Southern hemisphere, I was reminded of an incident that occurred during the early days in Taizé. I was walking back from a nearby village. On the road I passed a young man who bore the visible marks of poverty. A question struck me forcibly: will you ever be like him? Don't you always have someone to count on? Isn't poverty having no one to talk to when all else fails? Will you be alongside those who are as destitute as this? I was compelled to reply. I made my choice. Since then I have wondered: who was it that I met? Today I think I know. In that man, Christ was present as much as he possibly could be.

Inner Life and Human Solidarities

If you want to carry a fire right into the darkest nights of humanity, will you let an inner life grow, deep within you? A life with neither beginning nor end. A land on fire. Then you would become a leaven of trust and peace even where the human community is torn apart, in its deserts. Across the earth, so many others, believers and non-believers, are already striving to be a leaven of trust between peoples. Seeking healing for the divisions between South and North, between East and West, they stand out as signs of what we hardly dared hope for.

Brother Roger and a few brothers go each year to spend time in a poor district of a city on a Southern continent, as here in Calcutta.

We have come to live in a district of Calcutta to be among those who are familiar with the most prevalent condition on earth, poverty. The nights are short, the street noises intense. In two or three days, a simplification of our life-style has taken place. The people of the neighbourhood are surprised that foreigners are willing to sleep on the ground.

Work in the home for the dying. Here, what can we give except first and foremost human love? Going from one to another, stopping to spend a few moments with each one, telling them that they are our brothers, our friends or, the youngest, our children.

In Calcutta, there are visible homes for the dying. In Western civilization, many of the young people are in homes for the dying that are invisible but none the less real; marked by human abandonment, broken family relationships which affect them to their very depths, they are like the living dead. And there are old people who are forced to end their lives in isolation. It is as if they had nothing else before them but to wait for death. Who will kiss their worn hands when the meaning of their life vanishes from their eyes?

In front of the shack in Mathare Valley.

Nairobi. The area we wanted to live in is called Mathare Valley. It is the biggest slum in the city. The poorest in all of Africa, some say. A hundred thousand people are piled up on the slope of a small valley. People kept on telling us it was a dangerous district, where fear, violence, drunkenness and theft were rife and it would be impossible to stay. No white had ever lived in Mathare Valley.

We stayed for over a month and it was not easy to say goodbye to the residents of the district. They were so welcoming. Happily some of my brothers stayed on in the same shack for several years.

Why share in this way the life of the most neglected? It is not a question of personal taste, nor of a natural inclination; it is to allow the most trying human conditions to enter into our own lives. How can we appeal for solidarity with the poor while staying at home and doing nothing?

When some of my brothers live for years among the poorest of the poor, that presence is never a revival of the process which involves coming from the Northern hemisphere and bringing our own imported solutions, no matter how valuable they may be. We know all too well how wary the inhabitants of the Southern hemisphere are of any relationship of dependency. If we go to these places, it is in order to live a presence with no ulterior motives.

To the question 'Do we go with absolutely no intention of accomplishing anything?' we would answer 'No'. Though we do not seek short-term results by bringing money or solutions worked out in the West, we do want to support local young people who are taking initiatives inspired by their own culture and their own genius, arising from the very depths of their own peoples. Such young men and women exist. They have concrete suggestions to offer. Like young Europeans, they are sometimes discouraged in the face of impossibilities, and in danger of falling into a scepticism which will lead them either to passivity or to violence.

We go to live with them in slums, above all to live a parable of communion, always with only a minimum of material resources. And this in the presence of the reserved Sacrament, which turns a run-down shack into a place inhabited by a Presence. Immersing ourselves in slums means living in the same way as the inhabitants, and waiting with them for an event from God for their peoples.

Cape Town, South Africa. In a black neighbourhood called Crossroads, a whole crowd had gathered for prayer. They were singing. Human voices can express the call from the depths more powerfully than anything else.

They welcomed us and handed me the microphone. I alluded to an African man of God my parents met one day when I was five years old. He had blessed me. After that my mother often used to say 'In Europe the faith is disappearing, but the Gospel in all its freshness will come back from Africa'. I assured them that today that blessing of long ago was finding fulfilment.

Then someone else spoke. But I said to myself: my words were so inadequate. I asked the two brothers who were there if I should take the microphone once more. They said yes. I tried then to express all that was in my heart by a gesture. I explained to the Africans: 'I would like to ask you for forgiveness, not in the name of the whites, I could not do that, but because you are suffering for the Gospel and you go before us into the Kingdom of God. I would like to pass from one to another of you so that each of you can make the sign of the cross on my palm, the sign of Christ's forgiveness.' The gesture was understood immediately. Everyone made it, even the children. It seemed to take an eternity. Spontaneously they burst into songs of resurrection.

In sub-Saharan Africa.

Throughout the world, the innocence of the very young is often wounded when their most sincere intentions are distorted, when their love is rejected. At the end of a stay in Haiti, in a miserable shanty-town, a child who had nothing, not even a shred of clothing, insisted: 'Take me with you!' And the other children around him cried out: 'Yes, he has no mother or father'. In that slum, so many faces revealed each day a reflection of Christ on the cross.

In Haiti, we went several times to visit an old black woman who welcomes the poor and destitute in her home. One day this woman prayed, full of compassion: 'I suffer because as soon as we have helped one human being in distress, another is already here with more suffering'. To be truly alive means loving with a heartfelt compassion like that old woman.

There are also abandoned human beings in the Northern hemisphere but they are more hidden, less easily seen. Thus a young boy from a big city said about the parable of the prodigal son: 'In my family, I, the son, didn't go away; it was my father who left us'.

The risen Christ, who lives in the radiance of God, is at the same time in anguish, today, tomorrow and until the end of the world, with all those who are undergoing trials. To understand Jesus' death on the cross it is necessary first of all to grasp that he is risen, and that at every moment he comes to meet us just as we are. He comes down to the lowest point of our human condition. He takes upon himself all that hurts us. He is present for those who are forced to suffer a kind of little death by contempt and the violence of hatred.

In Haiti.

Living the Passover with Christ

A new symbol brought back from Moscow. On Friday evenings, lay the icon of the cross on the floor, go and place your forehead on the wood of the cross, entrust to God, by a prayer of the body, your own burdens and those of others. In this way be in communion with the risen Christ who stays by the side of those undergoing trials throughout the world.

If the young, once they are back home, met every week, faithfully throughout their lives, to pray with others around the cross, they would lead God's people to become a contemplative people.

Every Friday evening in Taizé there is prayer
around the cross. It is a way of expressing an
invisible communion not only with Christ on
the cross but with all who suffer, who are
abandoned, imprisoned, tortured, or
condemned to silence. It is a way of silently
entrusting to Christ our own burdens as well
as everything that weighs upon others, nearby
or afar—the oppressed, the helpless, the ill,
the persecuted. This prayer was started by
young people in Eastern Europe.

Lord Christ, even if we had faith great enough to move mountains, without living charity, what would we be?
You love us.

Without your Spirit who lives in our hearts, what would we be?
You love us.

By taking everything upon yourself, you open for us a way toward faith, toward trust in God, who wants neither suffering nor human distress.

Spirit of the risen Christ, Spirit of compassion, Spirit of praise, your love for each one will never disappear.

Spirit of the living God, when our doubts and hesitations to welcome you seem to submerge all else, you are there, present for every human being without exception.

You rekindle the fire smouldering within, beneath our ashes. You feed this fire with our own thorns and all that hurts us in ourselves and others, so that even the stones in our hearts can become glowing lights in our darkness, dawn in the depths of our night.

If you were not risen, O Christ, to whom could we go to find the radiance of God's own face?

If you were not risen, we would not be together seeking your communion. We would not find forgiveness and reconciliation at your side—those wellsprings of a new beginning.

If you were not risen, where could we draw the energies to follow you to the very end of our lives, choosing you again and again, until we enter eternity's life?

O living God, in our darkness you kindle a fire that never dies out.

By means of the spirit of praise, you draw us out of ourselves. To us, God's poor, you have entrusted a mystery of hope.

Within our human frailty you have set a spiritual force that never disappears. Even when we are not aware of it, it is always there, ready to carry us onwards. And even if our heart condemns us, you are so much greater than our heart.

Yes, in our darkness you kindle a fire that never dies out.

Every Saturday evening, a festival of the light of Christ is a way of celebrating the resurrection that already begins mysteriously here on earth for each of us. While a song of resurrection is sung, the tapers each person has received on entering are lit—a sign of the light of Christ, and a sign that as Christians we are called to be children of light.

In the Church of Reconciliation there is a
copy of this seventh-century Coptic icon from
Egypt: Christ with his arm round the shoulder
of a friend. By this gesture he takes upon
himself the burdens, the mistakes, all the
loads weighing down upon the other. Christ is
not shown facing his friend; he walks
alongside him, accompanying him. That
friend is each one of us.

Tirelessly, Christ seeks us out and is at work within us. He keeps on asking: do you love me? Do you love me more than anyone else? That is because our relationship with him is one of friendship. And just as all friendship knows periods of indifference, so too in our life there are times of indifference to Christ. No friendship can grow without new beginnings, reconciliations. When we let ourselves be reconciled with Christ, we discover him as if for the first time: the love of all loves, mistreated, wounded, rejected by many and yet never tired of accompanying us.

A Parable of Community

Brother, you trust in God's mercy: the Lord Christ, in his compassion and his love for you, has chosen you to be in the Church a sign of brotherly love. It is his will that with your brothers you live the parable of community.

So, refusing to look back, and joyful with infinite gratitude, never fear to outstrip the dawn, praising, blessing and singing Christ your Lord.

Faced with the urgent need to make the Gospel present at the heart of the human family, we are aware how limited the resources of our community are when compared with the vast horizons opening out in this eve of a new millennium.

What are you, little community? An efficient instrument? No. Never. Fine as that might be.

Perhaps a group of men united to be stronger, humanly speaking, in order to realize their own aims? Not that either.

So could we be living a common life in order to be comfortable together? No. The community would then become an end in itself, and that would allow us to settle down in cosy little nests. Being happy together? Certainly, but in the context of the offering of our lives.

What are you, little community, spread out in different parts of the world? A parable of communion, a simple reflection of that unique communion which is the Body of Christ, his Church, and therefore a leaven in the human family.

What is your calling? In our common life, we can only move forward by discovering ever anew the miracle of love, in daily forgiveness, heartfelt trust, and peace-filled contemplation of those entrusted to us. When we move away from the miracle of love all is lost, everything comes apart.

Little community, what might be God's desire for you? To be made alive by drawing nearer to the holiness of Christ.

Young brothers meeting in Brother Roger's
room. The community is made up of some
ninety brothers, both Catholic and from
various Protestant backgrounds, and from
more than twenty nations.

Who can grasp all that a look conveys? I listen to a brother. One word hesitantly follows another. If there were only words, I should be unable to understand completely. But in his eyes there shines a fierce struggle, the refusal to serve himself at another's expense.

This morning, during the common prayer, all at once I became aware of the quality of my brothers and I was moved to the depths of my heart. They give their lives—their whole lives. They pay a dear price for their commitment. I know that better than any. Then I can no longer say if my admiration is for my brothers or for Christ who has so set his mark upon them.

Brother Roger with Marie-Sonaly, his god-daughter.

Will you, for love of Christ, consecrate yourself to him with all your being?—I will.

Will you henceforth fulfil your service of God within our community, in communion with your brothers?—I will.

Will you, renouncing all ownership, live with your brothers not only in community of material goods but also in community of spiritual goods, striving for openness of heart?—I will.

Will you, in order to be more available to serve with your brothers, and in order to give yourself in undivided love to Christ, remain in celibacy?—I will.

Will you, so that we may be of one heart and one mind and so that the unity of our common service may be fully achieved, adopt the orientations of the community expressed by the servant of communion, bearing in mind that he is only a poor servant in the community?—I will.

Will you, always discerning Christ in your brothers, watch over them in good days and bad, in suffering and joy? —I will.

After three or four years of preparation, each
brother takes monastic commitments for life.
The Spirit of God is invoked upon the new
brother.

Brother, from now on your worship and your service are integrated in a brotherly community, itself set in the body of the Church. In the inner searching so necessary for your Christian life, you are stimulated by others' dynamism. You are not alone any more. Your brothers are to be considered in everything.

The Lord Christ comes to help the weakness of your faith; committing himself with you, he fulfils for you his promise: Truly, there is no one who has given up home, brothers, sisters, mother, father, wife or children for my sake and the Gospel's, who will not receive a hundred times as much at present—homes and brothers and sisters and mothers and children—and persecutions too, and in the age to come eternal life.

This is a way contrary to all human reason; like Abraham you can only advance along it by faith, not by sight, always sure that whoever loses his life for Christ's sake will find it.

From now on walk in the steps of Christ. Do not be anxious about tomorrow. First seek God's Kingdom and its justice. Surrender yourself, give yourself, and good measure, pressed down, shaken together, brimming over, will be poured out for you; the measure you give is the measure you will receive.

Never let your inner life make you look sad, like someone who puts on a grief-stricken air to attract attention. Anoint your head and wash your face, so that only your Father who is in secret knows what your heart intends.

Be concerned to establish communion with your neighbour.

At the foot of the
hill, close to an
ancient spring, there
is a hermitage where
brothers often go to
pray.

Lord Christ, gentle and humble of heart, we hear your quiet call: 'You, follow me'.

You give us this vocation so that together we may live a parable of communion and, having taken the risk of an entire lifetime, we may be a leaven of reconciliation in that irreplaceable communion called the Church.

Show us how to respond courageously, without getting trapped in the quicksand of our hesitations. Come, so that we may be sustained by the breath of your Spirit, the one thing that matters, without which nothing impels us to keep on moving forward.

You ask all who know how to love and suffer with you to leave themselves behind and follow you. When, to love with you and not without you, we must abandon some project contrary to your plan, then come, O Christ, and fill us with quiet confidence: make us realize that your love will never disappear, and that to follow you means giving our lives.

At the hermitage of the living spring.

WWW.THECREATIVEWRITERS

Lorem ipsum dolor sit amet, consectetuer adipiscing elit. Aenean commodo ligula eget dolor. Aenean massa. Cum sociis natoque penatibus et magnis dis parturient montes, nascetur ridiculus mus. Donec quam felis, ultricies nec, pellentesque eu, pretium quis, sem. Nulla consequat massa quis enim. Donec pede justo, fringilla vel, aliquet nec, vulputate eget, arcu. In enim justo, rhoncus ut, imperdiet a, venenatis vitae, justo.

Unblock creativity, enhance imagination and learn the *art* of story creation as you write fiction, personal memoir and poetry.

Be inspired...write your story!

Web : www.thecreativewritersworkshop.com

Email: creativewriting@ireland.com   Tel: +353 (0)86 252 3428

THE CREATI... WRITER WORKS!

Founder: Iren...

Est: 1991

A brother in his room.
A community meal.

Be a sign for others of joy and brotherly love. Open yourself to all that is human and you will find that every vain desire to escape from the world disappears. Be present to your age; adapt yourself to the conditions of the moment. Father, I pray you, not to take them out of the world, but to keep them from evil. Love the deprived, all who are suffering from injustice and thirsting for justice. Jesus had special concern for them. Never be afraid of their bothering you.

Love your neighbours, whatever their religious or ideological point of view. Never resign yourself to the scandal of the separation of Christians, all so readily professing love for their neighbour, yet remaining divided. Make the unity of Christ's Body your passionate concern.

To have brothers in far-away countries, sharing the living conditions of people in sub-human situations, is like seeing the flesh of our flesh become part of the poorest of peoples.

Wrote to one of them: 'If we had no presence such as yours in the slum in which you live, the holiness of Christ for which we are striving might well be a holy life, but one turned in upon itself. Where then would the thrust towards the catholicity of the Church be? As never before, you are advancing along that road. Through the life you are living, we are not leaving the worst casualties in the human family to their fate.'

Wrote to another brother, on another continent: 'If the pen were to express our communion, I would need to write you in letters of flame'. In the midst of all the contradictions in which our vocation places us, this brother's courage carries me onwards.

The brothers do not all live in Taizé. Some, in
small groups, share in great simplicity the
living conditions of poor districts in North
and South America, Africa and Asia.

For our community, to have brothers from distant continents is both a fulfilment and a beginning.

It is the fulfilment of a sign of universality we were waiting for, more indispensable today than in the past, for we know know how hard it is to insert a leaven of communion into the heart of the human family. These young men, our brothers, leave their families, their countries. They set out like Abraham, who 'did not know where he was going'. They accomplish a sheer act of faith beyond all human explanations. In their countries of origin the West often represents a power to be feared.

The boundless trust of these men urges us on. Then their presence becomes a beginning. We would like, not to welcome them, but to allow Christ, through them, to welcome us.

The community, in Taizé and elsewhere, has
no capital in reserve. The brothers accept no
gifts or donations, not even personal
inheritances. They live from their work alone.

To the Wellsprings of Faith

'One passes through Taizé as one passes close to a spring of water.'
(*Pope John Paul II in Taizé*)

Even during the great summer meetings, in Taizé there are places of quiet and solitude to retreat to.

Beside the Church of Reconciliation there is a chapel where a spring of water flows, a reminder of baptism, of Christ's forgiveness, a humble place of prayer for inner healing.

Where would we be today, if women, men and even children had not come forward at times when humanity seemed to be heading for the worst? They held on to a fine hope in humanity and to an invisible presence. They found a way to go beyond personal conflicts and cross the barriers which separate nations and people of different spiritual families or races.

Are you going to let yourself sink into discouragement like Elijah, a believer of times past who, convinced that he could do nothing more for his people, lay down under a tree to fall asleep and forget? Or will you take your place among those women, men and children who have decided to act?

As you seek to follow Jesus Christ, could it be that you find yourself alone, cast into a kind of human desert, without anyone with whom you can share the trust of faith?

The Risen One comes to wrest you away from loneliness by letting you rely on the trust of his witnesses, from Mary and the Apostles to those of the present day. So this can be your prayer: 'Lord Christ, enable me to be a living member in that mystery of communion which is the Church; enable me, day after day, to dispose myself inwardly to place my trust in the Mystery of Faith. O Christ, look not on my sins but on the faith of your Church.'

What you were unable to accomplish by yourself becomes possible in this communion . . . and the holiness of Christ is no longer out of reach, it is quite close to you . . . within you.

In a great diversity of languages, experiences and backgrounds, all are called to listen and to learn from the gifts of others. Every morning Bible introductions are given by brothers of the community.

Those who wish can spend the whole week in silence.

Throughout the day and even at
night, young people pray in
silence in the Church of
Reconciliation as well as in the
twelfth-century village church. The
reserved Sacrament is kept in both
of these places of prayer.

Very often a single man or woman who dared to pray alone in a church became, by persevering, a living call for others. Just one person is enough for many others to be brought along one day.

Can you perceive it? Can you discern it? When your night becomes dark, God's love is a fire. Perhaps the fire is under the ashes and no longer gives light. Perhaps, overcome by doubt, you are asking yourself: but where is God? Could he remain silent?

Never absent from your life, the Spirit of the Risen Lord is always in you. Knowing this is enough to keep you wakeful. And through humble trust in him, light breaks through into your night.

If my brothers and I kept our eyes only on what we see in Taizé, we could be enthusiastic. So many young people come to our hillside, even in winter. We notice their thirst for prayer, the hours they spend in church, with or without us!

When we travel, however, preparing for meetings in very different countries, we realize that many are seeking Christ, but taking him in isolation; Christ in the communion of his Body is being abandoned. The sense of the mystery of the Church is vanishing.

If there were not this abandonment of Christ in the communion of his Body, his Church, we would not invest so much energy, my brothers and I, in gathering young people together and searching with them, not only at Taizé, but also elsewhere, across Western and Eastern Europe, or on other continents.

Those who have come to Taizé return home to share their experiences with others. They form no organized movement. All are called to become involved where they live, particularly in their local parish or congregation, and to build up trust between people of different generations, between divided Christians and between people of different cultures.

Those from the Southern continents, who come from lands where faith is often more alive, can contribute to a new evangelization of Europe, to a springtime of the Church. After a period of preparation in Taizé, they go with young Europeans to spend a few weeks in the parishes of Europe.

During the Rome meeting a prayer service was
held with Pope John Paul II in St Peter's
Basilica.

On Sunday, 5 October 1986, Pope John Paul
II visited Taizé during a trip to France. He
had already been to Taizé twice as Archbishop
of Cracow. The Pope took part in a prayer in
the Church of Reconciliation, where
thousands of young people who had gathered
around the community were waiting for him;
then he met with the brothers for a
conversation.

Words of Pope John Paul II to the community:

Dear Brothers, in the family-like intimacy of this brief meeting, I would like to express to you my affection and my trust with these simple words, with which Pope John XXIII, who loved you so much greeted Brother Roger one day: 'Ah, Taizé, that little springtime!'

My desire is that the Lord may keep you like a springtime that blossoms.

Although you did not look for it, you have seen young people from everywhere come to you by the thousands, attracted by your prayer and your community life. How can we not think that these young people are the gift and the means the Lord gives you to stimulate you to remain together, in the joy and the freshness of your gift, as a springtime for all who are searching for true life?

I do not forget that in its unique, original and in a certain sense provisional vocation, your community can awaken astonishment and encounter incomprehension and suspicion. But because of your passion for the reconciliation of all Christians in a full communion, because of your love for the Church, you will be able to continue, I am sure, to be open to the will of the Lord.

By desiring to be yourselves a 'parable of community', you will help all whom you meet to be faithful to their church affiliation, the fruit of their education and their choice in conscience, but also to enter more and more deeply into the mystery of communion that the Church is in God's plan. By his Gift to his Church, Christ liberates forces of love in all Christians and gives them a universal heart to be creators of justice and peace, able to unite to their contemplation a struggle along the lines of the Gospel for the integral liberation of human beings, of every human being and of the entire human being.

Church, become what you are in your depths: a land of the living, a land of reconciliation, a land of simplicity.

Church, land of the living, open the doors to an inner life, that everyone may be not half-dead but fully alive. Throw open the doors to joy. Enable us to glimpse something of heaven's joy on earth by means of an all-embracing, meditative prayer, which gathers together people of all ages, and where the singing never comes to an end.

Church, be a land of reconciliation. There will never be a widespread awakening of Christians unless they live as people who are reconciled. Once you are transfigured by a reconciliation which is not put off until later, you will be a leaven of trust and peace between peoples.

For years now, young people from Eastern Europe have been coming to the meetings in Taizé. For years too, Brother Roger and other brothers have gone to lead meetings in Eastern Europe, but without the participation of young Western Europeans. In 1987, for the first time, a meeting in Eastern Europe was open to young people from the West. It was held in Ljubljana, Yugoslavia. In the common prayers, Slavonic languages were in the majority: Polish, Slovene, Serbo-Croatian, Macedonian, Russian. Prayers were also sung or spoken in Hungarian and Albanian.

Church, be a land of simplicity. The use of simple means promotes a life of communion, whereas exterior signs of power undermine trust and arouse fear. Do not forget the hopes of so many people who are deeply concerned that a way be found to share the world's wealth more fairly. The inequality which exists is one of the sources of armed conflict. Be a land of sharing in order to be a land of peace.

In addition to the European meetings and the
East–West meetings, the Pilgrimage of Trust
on Earth also includes other gatherings, in
cities on different continents—Montreal, New
York, Santo Domingo, Brussels, Dublin,
Madrid, East Berlin, Warsaw, and so on.
There are also intercontinental meetings like
this one in Madras, where common prayer was
celebrated in a temporary cathedral of
bamboo.

If festivity faded away from the Body of Christ, the Church, that spirit of festival still so alive in the depths of the peoples of the Southern continents, where on the earth could there still be found a place of communion for all humanity?

When this communion is rendered transparent by reconciliations, by forgiveness, by the struggle of love, there is nothing left in it to veil the reflection on human faces of the face of the Risen Christ. The Holy Spirit keeps watch within you: a shaft of light into the dark nights. And the doors of a communion open up. Will you seek there the vitality to keep you in solidarity with the wounds of the human family? . . . Do not be afraid, trust is at hand, and with it a happiness.

Some Important Dates

1940: On 20 August, Brother Roger, 25 years old, arrives in Taizé and chooses this village as the home for the future community.

Alone for two years, he gives shelter to political refugees, mostly Jews.

1949: At Easter, in the village church, the first seven brothers commit themselves for life to celibacy and common life.

At the suggestion of Cardinal Gerlier of Lyons, first journey to Rome; audience with Pope Pius XII.

1951: First group of brothers living outside Taizé. Through the years, other 'fraternities' follow (not foundations but provisional presences) on every continent, in places of poverty and division.

1953: Brother Roger finishes writing 'The Rule of Taizé'.

1958–1963: Annual audiences with Pope John XXIII. During the final one, the Pope opens up a whole new perspective with his words concerning the Church.

1959: Construction of guest accommodation four kilometres from Taizé to house young adults coming in ever greater numbers. It soon proves to be too small and too far away.

1960 and 1961: For the first time since the Reformation, at the invitation of Taizé, meetings for Catholic Bishops and Protestant Pastors. They spend three days on the hill.

1962: Inauguration of the Church of Reconciliation. Nine years later the rear wall has to be demolished and a large tent added to make it larger.

First visit by a brother to East Germany.

1962–1965: Invitation to take part in Second Vatican Council. Several brothers spend three months in Rome each year.

1963: Paul VI becomes Pope; he has known Taizé for almost fifteen years.

1966: More and more young adults in Taizé; first international youth gathering.

The Sisters of St Andrew, an international Catholic community founded in the thirteenth century, come to help with the work of welcoming people.

1968: Six brothers attend the General Assembly of the World Council of Churches in Uppsala, Sweden.

1969: Brother Roger includes pages from his journal in *Violent for Peace*. Subsequently, a volume of his journal appears every two or three years.

The first Catholic brothers enter the community.

1970: At Easter, announcement of the Worldwide Council of Youth. Young people make visits on five continents. The week-long youth meetings in Taizé gradually extend throughout the year, even in winter.

1973: The Archbishop of Canterbury, Dr Michael Ramsey, visits Taizé.

First meeting of young people in Poland.

1974: Opening of the Worldwide Council of Youth. The Pope, the Patriarch of Constantinople, the Archbishop of Canterbury and several Protestant Churches send representatives.

Brother Roger receives the Templeton Prize in London from Prince Philip 'for widening and deepening man's knowledge and love of God through his worldwide work among young people and his efforts for renewal and reconciliation'.

1975: Brother Roger in Chile shortly after the coup d'état.

1976: In a poor district of Calcutta, Brother Roger and an intercontinental team write a 'Letter to the People of God' on the theme of sharing. From then on, Brother Roger writes a letter at the end of each year.

1977: 'Letter to All the Generations' written among the poor living on junks in the South China Sea in Hong Kong.

1978: 'Letter from Africa' written in a slum in Kenya. Visit to South Africa.

First European Meeting in Paris. From here on, at each year's end, a European Meeting brings together 20,000 to 25,000 young people in Rome, London, Paris, Barcelona or Cologne.

1979: 'Itinerary for a Pilgrim' written during a stay with the poor in Chile. The expression 'Council of Youth' is set aside for a time, to be replaced by the Pilgrimage of Trust on Earth animated by young people but open to all generations.

1980: Meetings in the United States (New York, Washington) and in Canada (Montreal, Ottawa, Toronto).
First meeting of young people in East Germany.
First European Meeting in Rome, with 25,000 participants. Prayer in St Peter's with Pope John Paul II.
'Letter from Italy'.

1981: First European Meeting in London. Seventeen thousand young Europeans cross the Channel in one night to take part. Prayers in St Paul's Cathedral, Westminster Cathedral and Westminster Abbey. 'Letter from Warsaw'. Brother Roger visits Northern Ireland. He plans to spend Christmas in Poland, but the frontiers are suddenly closed on 13 December, and the 1,000 Poles planning to come to London are unable to attend.

1982: Stay in Lebanon. Beginning of 'The Pilgrimage of Trust on Earth'. 'Letter from the Catacombs'.

1983: Youth Meeting in Madrid; Brother Roger, accompanied by children, meets the American and Soviet ambassadors and brings them an appeal for peace. 'Letter from Haiti' published after a stay in a slum in Port-au-Prince.
Brothers in North America begin a series of pilgrimages which takes them to over sixty cities in four years.
In Taizé, Brother Roger and Mother Teresa make a common appeal for solidarity and reconciliation.

1984: Dr Robert Runcie, Archbishop of Canterbury, visits Taizé. Stay in sub-Saharan Africa. 'Letter from the Desert'.

1985: With children from five continents, Brother Roger brings to Javier Pérez de Cuéllar, Secretary-General of the United Nations, six questions from young people about peace and world disarmament.
Meeting in Dublin in the presence of Catholic and Protestant Church leaders, bringing together young people from the Republic of Ireland and Northern Ireland.
Intercontinental Meeting in Madras, India, with young people from 45 countries. 'Letter from Madras'.

1986: Pope John Paul II in Taizé: 'I want to express to you my affection and my trust with these simple words with which Pope John XXIII, who loved you so much, greeted Brother Roger one day: "Ah, Taizé, that little springtime!" ' And John Paul II added: 'One passes through Taizé as one passes close to a spring of water'.
Meetings in East Berlin and Warsaw.
Second European Meeting in London. Nineteen thousand young people from throughout Europe and beyond join young people from Britain and Ireland for several days of prayer and reflection. The Archbishop of Canterbury, Cardinal Hume and other Church leaders take part in the prayers.

1987: First East–West European Meeting, in Ljubljana, Yugoslavia.
From June to September, Intercontinental Youth Meetings in Taizé with 40,000 young people from almost 100 nations.
Third European Meeting in Rome, with 24,000 participants, including 5,000 from Eastern Europe: 'The Pope feels deeply involved in your pilgrimage of trust on earth'. 'Letter from Ethiopia'.

1988: From March to November, 33 Intercontinental Meetings in Taizé. Hundreds of young people from other continents, invited by Europeans, visit parishes and youth groups in Europe after a time of preparation in Taizé.
Brother Roger's second visit with UN Secretary-General Pérez de Cuéllar to hand over 'Suggestions from the young regarding the UN' on questions of sharing, peace and justice.
Brother Roger receives the UNESCO Prize for Peace Education.
Second Intercontinental Meeting in Madras.
European Meeting in Paris.
'Letter from Russia'.

1989: Taizé sends one million New Testaments in Russian to the Orthodox Church in Russia.
28 April to 1 May: East–West European Meeting in Hungary, attended by 20,000 young people.
For the first time, the big end-of-the-year European Meeting is held in Eastern Europe, in Wrocław, Poland.

1990: 24 to 27 May: first youth meeting in Scandinavia, in Linköping, Sweden.

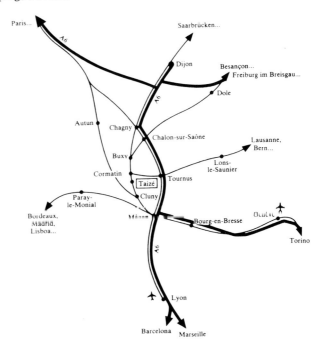

Additional Texts and Photographs of Taizé

During the winter of 1952–53 Brother Roger completed 'The Rule of Taizé'. He had already outlined its first features while he was still alone in Taizé and these were contained in a small booklet published in 1941. Thereafter, he wanted the Community to experience ten years or so of existence before drafting 'The Rule' where he indicates to his brothers 'the essentials for a common life'. His recent major revision of 'The Rule', along with four letters to young people, is to be published as *Living Springs* (UK: Mowbray).

Between 1958 and 1968, Brother Roger wrote a first series of books whose titles still sound like key-words, even if some of them are now out of print: *Living Today for God, Unity: Man's Tomorrow, The Dynamic of the Provisional, Unanimity in Pluralism* (which for a time was a commentary and actualization of 'The Rule'), *Violent for Peace*. These books are increasingly inspired by daily dialogue with ever growing numbers of young people. They gradually take the form of notes written day by day.

Festival without End was the first volume of Brother Roger's journal. Later, every two or three years, there followed: *Struggle and Contemplation, A Life We Never Dared Hope For, The Wonder of A Love, And Your Deserts Shall Flower, A Heart That Trusts*. In these books, pages from the journal alternate with dialogues, meditative texts and some of the prayers that Brother Roger writes each day for the common prayer at noon. (UK: Mowbray; USA: *Afire With Love: Meditations on Peace and Unity*, Crossroad, New York.)

In 1987, in the United States, a selection of texts from various writings by Brother Roger was brought together under the title *Awakened From Within: Meditations On The Christian Life* (Doubleday, New York).

Having met a number of times, in Calcutta, Taizé and Rome, Brother Roger and Mother Teresa have written jointly *The Way of the Cross* (India: ATC, Bangalore; UK: Mowbray; USA: The Pilgrim Press, New York) and *Mary, Mother of Reconciliations* (Australia: St Paul Publications, Homebush, NSW; India: Daughters of St Paul, Bombay; Philippines: Claretian Publications, Quezon City; UK: Mowbray; USA: Paulist Press, Mahwah, NJ).

At the end of each year, Brother Roger addresses a letter to young people, generally from a place where great poverty exists and where he is living for a time. These letters are translated into 26 languages and for a whole year they serve as the basis of the reflection in the Intercontinental Meetings at Taizé and for the Pilgrimage of Trust on Earth. The most recent of these have been published in booklet form: *Letter from the Desert, Letter from Madras, Letter from Ethiopia* and *Letter from Russia*. In the same series, there is an account of the visit of Pope John Paul II to Taizé, entitled *Passing by a Spring of Water* (Ateliers et Presses de Taizé).

First published in 1980 and subsequently revised and updated several times, *The Story of Taizé*, by Spanish author José Luis Gonzalez Balado, traces the vocation of the community from its beginnings right up to the Intercontinental Meetings held there throughout the summer of 1987 (UK: Mowbray).

Taizé: Trust, Forgiveness, Reconciliation is a booklet of photographs, with texts by Brother Roger and an account of a visit to Taizé (1983; UK: Mowbray).

In 1986, a detailed account of the life of Brother Roger, the community and the meetings for young adults was written by Kathryn Spink, who has also written biographies of John XXIII, John Paul II and Mother Teresa: *A Universal Heart: The Life and Vision of Brother Roger of Taizé* (UK: SPCK, London; USA: Harper & Row, New York).

Taizé: A Pilgrimage of Trust on Earth is a brief summary of the history and life of the community, the welcoming of young people from every continent, and the search with them to combine interior life and human solidarity, illustrated with colour photographs (Mowbray—Ateliers et Presses de Taizé).

The Letter from Taizé is published in nine languages every two months (Ateliers et Presses de Taizé).

Praying Together in Word and Song is a booklet based on the Taizé experience. As well as nearly 30 chants and songs from Taizé, it contains sections on meditative singing, verses from the psalms, Bible readings, silence and intercessions. All these can be used for personal prayer, prayer in groups or the Sunday parish celebration (1988; UK: Mowbray; USA: GIA Publications, Chicago, IL).

Music from Taizé (2 volumes): vocal and instrumental editions. (Australia: Dove Communications, Blackburn, Vic.; UK: Collins Religious Publishing, London; USA: GIA).

Taizé—That Little Springtime: a VHS video documentary (UK: Mowbray; USA: Journey Communications, Mount Vernon, VA).

Taizé: Trust Is At Hand: a 28-minute VHS videocassette, made at Taizé; showing also 'Taizé outside Taizé' (UK: Mowbray).

Cassettes of music and songs from Taizé: Distribution: Auvidis, Paris (Australia: Rainbow Book Agencies, Richmond, Vic.; UK: various religious bookshops; USA: GIA).